CONTENTS

KU-078-539

INTRODUCTION TO INDONESIA

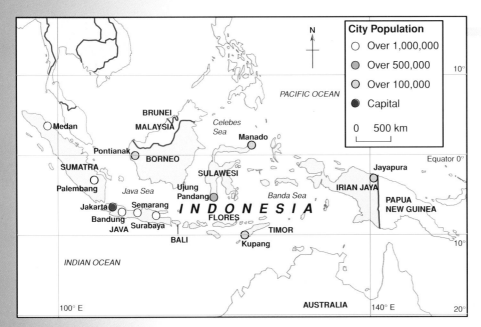

Indonesia: towns and population

COUNTRY OF ISLANDS

Indonesia is a country in the south-east of Asia. It is made up of lots of islands. Some are big but others are so small that nobody lives on them. These islands are spread over 5000 km, from east to west.

In the Middle Ages, traders from Europe used to travel to the Sulawesi Islands in Indonesia to buy spices. Then the islands were called the Spice Islands.

Bowls of spices and other foods on sale in a market.

HISTORY

In the last 400 years, different countries have ruled in parts of Indonesia. Since 1945, it has been ruled by its own **government** and has its own president.

LIVING TOGETHER

There are just over 200 million people in Indonesia. They have different religions and different ways of life. There are 250 different languages.

Indonesia's name may come from two old words in a language of the area. Indos meant 'islands' and nesos meant 'trade'.

Jakarta is the **capital city** of Indonesia. There are many modern buildings and roads in the city centre.

THE LAND

ISLANDS AND OCEANS

Indonesia's islands are spread over a large area of the Pacific and Indian oceans. Between the islands there are narrow areas of sea called **straits**.

MOUNTAINS

Most of the islands in Indonesia have mountains. None of them has much low or flat land. Many of the mountains are **volcanoes**. Some still **erupt** and send out hot **ashes** and **lava**. These are **active** volcanoes. There are also the remains of **extinct** volcanoes.

Indonesia: natural features

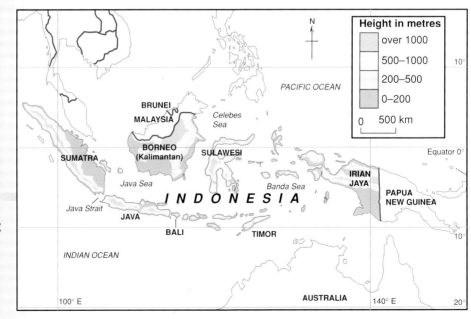

There are many volcanoes on the islands of Indonesia. Some of them still erupt. Farmers grow rice on the flat fields.

DISASTER

In 1883, there was a terrible disaster. A volcano on the island of Krakatoa blew itself apart. Krakatoa is between Java and Sumatra. The explosion caused very high waves on the sea, and thousands on people on Java and Sumatra were killed.

Parts of the ocean around Indonesia are very deep. One part called the Java Deep Trench is nearly 8 kilometres deep.

Rivers flow down to the seas from the mountains. This river is flowing through a mangrove forest near the coast.

7

WEATHER, PLANTS AND ANIMALS

HOT AND WET

Parts of Indonesia are on the **equator**. On the islands close to the equator, the weather is hot and it rains every day.

MONSOONS

Further away from the equator, part of the year is hot and dry and part is wet and warm. This is because winds, called **monsoons**, blow air from different directions at different times of the year.

Trees grow very tall to reach the light in this rain forest. They grow quickly in the hot and wet **climate**.

The Komodo Dragon is the world's biggest lizard. It lives in Komodo Island.

FORESTS AND WILDLIFE

Thousands of different plants grow in Indonesia. Just over half of Indonesia is covered by **rainforest**. There are trees such as teak, bamboo and palms. There are also creepers, orchids and other wild flowers.

There are colourful birds, insects, snakes and many other animals living in the forests. Some animals, such as monkeys, live in the trees. Since people started to cut down the trees in the rainforests, some of the animals have become very rare.

The world's biggest flower grows on the island of Sumatra. It grows to a metre across. It has a very nasty smell. It is called the Fragile Fantasy Flower.

9

VILLAGES AND CITIES

These houses are on the island of Sulawesi.

VILLAGE PEOPLE

Most people in Indonesia live in villages. Their houses are built from bamboo and other types of wood. The roof is either straw or sheets of iron. Floor mats and parts of the walls are made from coconut fibres.

THE CAPITAL CITY

Fewer than half the people live in towns and cities. Jakarta is the **capital city**. This is the biggest city. It has over 8 million people and many important buildings. The **government** and most of Indonesia's very important buildings are in Jakarta.

BUILDINGS IN JAKARTA

Some buildings in Jakarta are old. They were built by the Dutch and British when they ruled Indonesia. There are also modern office blocks, shops, flats and new factories.

*Groups of very poor homes are called **shanty towns**.*

HOMES FROM SCRAP

Poor people build their homes out of scrap wood and other materials. Most of them do not have clean water, electricity, drains or sewers.

Many people live in very poor houses in Jakarta. They catch diseases from the dirty water. They build their own houses and slowly make them better.

A CITY FAMILY

The Hartje family outside their home in Jakarta.

MEET THE HARTJE FAMILY

Mr and Mrs Hartje and their two children live in Jakarta. The children are called Jennifer and Joshua. Jennifer is thirteen years old. Joshua is three. They live in a house in one of the better parts of Jakarta.

OFF TO WORK

Mr and Mrs Hartje both go to work every day. He works in an office. She teaches English in a school. Jennifer goes to school with her mother, who is also one of her teachers. Joshua stays with some of the family's relations who live nearby.

A local mosque in the Pusat district of Jakarta. A mosque is where Muslims go to pray. Most people in Indonesia are Muslims.

CHILDREN AT SCHOOL

The children in Jennifer's school all wear school uniform. They sit at their desks in straight rows. The classrooms look very bare. Lessons start at 7.00 in the morning and end at 12.30. After lessons, Jennifer stays in school to play basketball and rounders.

Children in a classroom in Jennifer's school.

SHOPPING

Mrs Hartje shops in supermarkets, local shops and street markets. She buys rice, meat, prawns, vegetables and spices.

Mrs Hartje buying fruit in a street market.

The small three-wheeled taxi is used to take the shopping home.

FARMING IN INDONESIA

WORK ON FARMS

Most farms in Indonesia are small, with only a few fields. Farmers grow enough food for their families to live on. They sometimes have some extra food to sell.

GROWING RICE

The main crop is rice. This is grown in flat **paddy fields**. Farmers have to flood the fields for the rice to grow.

Oxen are used to do the heavy farm work.

This boy has caught some fish for his family to eat. What do you think the basket on his head is for?

OTHER FOODS

Farmers grow maize, soybeans, coconuts and vegetables. They also rear pigs, cattle and chickens. Spices are grown to add strong flavours to the food. People who live near the coast or by rivers catch fish.

CLEARING

Some farmers cut down trees to get more farm land. They grow crops on the **plot** until the soil becomes useless. Then they leave that plot and cut down more forest. The **government** wants them to stop doing this before the forest is all gone.

Just over half of the people in Indonesia work in farming.

A COUNTRY FAMILY

MEET THE TOTOK FAMILY

The Totok family live in a small town about 60 km from Jakarta. Mr and Mrs Totok have two children. Aryo is the older boy. He is twelve years old. Satria, his younger brother, is nine.

Mr Totok works for the **government** so he has a well-paid job. The family live in a big house.

The Totok family live in a big house in the town of **Bogor**.

Mr and Mrs Totok eating a meal at lunch time. They eat meals with their fingers.

Mrs Totok goes to this supermarket to buy food.

Aryo and Satria go to this school. The children sit outside in the shade for some lessons.

THE CHILDREN'S SCHOOL

Aryo and Satria both go to the same school. There are no walls and no doors on the classrooms. This is because it is so hot. There is a fan to help keep them cool. They have some lessons sitting outside under the shade of a **veranda**.

FAVOURITE SPORTS

The boys enjoy sports and other activities at their school. Their favourite sport is football. They watch English premier league matches on television on Saturday night. They also learn judo and karate.

These boys are learning karate at school. Karate is a way to defend yourself.

MARKETS AND SHOPS

MARKETS

Most people do their shopping in street markets. These are held in small country towns all over Indonesia. Women bring food from their farms to sell. Some bring pots, baskets and other **craft goods** they have made. People in the cities also shop in street markets. Some sell food, clothes and other everyday things. There are markets for electrical goods, watches and even one for tropical song birds.

Shops in a shopping mall in Jakarta the **capital city**. This is where wealthy people come to do their shopping.

Farmers bring food to sell in street markets. People in the cities often shop in these markets.

A GOOD DEAL

The buyer and seller always argue until they agree on a price. People are very good at getting the best prices.

SMART SHOPS

The modern shops are in the big cities. In Jakarta, there are department stores and shopping malls, as in any other big city around the world. The wealthy people come to do their shopping in these shops.

The main market in Banjarmasin city is held on small boats. People row from one boat to another to buy their goods.

INDONESIAN FOOD

EVERYDAY FOOD

Indonesian people mostly eat rice, maize and vegetables. The food is either boiled in a pot, or stirred and fried in an open pan called a wok.

HOT AND SPICY

People use all kinds of spices when they are cooking food. These include cloves, nutmegs, ginger, peppers and cinnamon. The spices make the food taste very hot.

This is how most people in Indonesia cook their meals. Rice is the main food that people eat.

A family eating in a restaurant. Can you see what kind of foods they are eating?

DIPS AND SAUCES

Food is often dipped into a spicy shrimp paste called *trasi*. Sauces are made from coconut milk, peanuts and soya beans.

SPECIAL DISHES

Lamb, pork and chicken are roasted on a spit over a barbecue. *Nasi goreng* is a meal made from eggs, meat, rice and vegetables. First, the eggs are used to make an omelette. Then chunks of beef or chicken are put into a wok with the omelette. Rice and vegetables are stirred in and the food is fried until it is ready.

Indonesians usually eat sitting on the ground. They mostly eat with the fingers of their right hands. Sometimes they use a spoon or fork instead.

MADE IN INDONESIA

Rubber is called latex. The man is cutting the bark to let the latex drip into a pot. This is called rubber tapping.

WHAT IS MADE?

There is a good chance that you own or use something that was made in Indonesia. It may be your clothes or sports shoes or parts in a computer.

INDONESIA'S RESOURCES

Wood from forests is made into paper, cardboard and chipboard. Oil and gas give chemicals and energy for factories and homes. Copper and other metals are mined and sold to other countries.

FACTORY WORKERS

Only a few people work in factories. They earn very little money compared to factory workers in wealthier countries. Sometimes children have to work too.

IS IT FAIR?

Goods you buy that are made in Indonesia may be cheap. This is because the workers are not paid much. Do you think this is fair?

Nike sports shoes are made in Indonesia.

These women are working in a factory that makes cloth. More people are working in factories than in the past.

GETTING AROUND

There are some very bad roads in Indonesia. The heavy rain can wash bridges away. Look at the holes in the road surface.

WALKING EVERYWHERE

More than half the people in Indonesia live in the countryside. They walk to their fields, walk to get water and walk to the nearest town. They may use an ox or donkey to pull a cart.

ON THE ROADS

There are some main roads with hard all-weather surfaces. Most roads are rough tracks that are not suitable for cars. Heavy rain can make roads impossible to use.

TRAINS AND BOATS

There are not many railway lines in Indonesia. It is hard to build railway lines through mountains and across steep valleys. Ferry boats take people across to other islands.

CITY JAMS

In the cities, people travel in cars, buses and colourful minivans. There are also tricycles with motors and rickshaws with pedals. The roads are very crowded.

Indonesians use the words jam kare to mean that time stretches like rubber. Things do not always happen at the right times.

Ferry boats sail between the islands. How many trucks do you think would fit on this boat?

ARTS AND SPORT

MAKING MUSIC

Traditional Indonesian orchestras play music on flutes, gongs and xylophones. These are called *gamelan* orchestras. Flutes are made from bamboo. Other instruments are made from wood and metal.

DANCING AND PLAYS

People who go to Indonesian islands love to watch the people dancing and making music. Dancers make slow and graceful movements to quiet music. Other types of entertainment are shadow plays and puppet plays. The puppets, called marionettes, are worked by wires.

This man is carving a figure to sell to tourists.

These dancers on Java are wearing masks. Look at the orchestra in the background. What instruments can you see?

VILLAGE CRAFTS

People make **craft goods**, such as baskets from rice straw, or mats from coconut fibres. Some make pictures and patterns on cloth, using hot wax. This is called batik.

SPORTS

Sports, such as badminton and football, have become popular. Indonesia also has its own type of **martial arts**. This is a way to defend yourself, using your hands or a stick.

About 4 million tourists go to Indonesia on holiday every year.

FESTIVALS AND CUSTOMS

MUSLIM FESTIVALS

A large number of Indonesians are Muslims. They pray in buildings called mosques and take part in holy festivals, such as Id-ul-Fitr and Ramadan.

FESTIVALS ON BALI

Most people who live on Bali are Hindus. Women sometimes walk in procession to their holy places or shrines, carrying gifts on their heads. The barong dance tells a story about an evil witch who is always beaten. Dancers dressed as monsters sometimes leap onto the stage.

The dancer makes slow and graceful movements. This is a dance about how good fights evil, on the island of Bali. It is called the barong dance.

Women taking gifts to a Hindu temple on Bali.

LOCAL FESTIVALS

There are many ancient festivals and customs in Indonesia. Weddings are special events. On the island of Flores, gifts are given to the bride's family as a payment. The village men then attack each other to show the women how brave they are.

WOMEN RULE

In one tribe on Sumatra, the women make all the decisions. They ask the men to marry them, and they own the land.

Indonesia has a National day on 17 August every year. Everyone from the different islands can feel that they belong to one country.

INDONESIA FACTFILE

People

People from Indonesia are called Indonesians.

Capital city

The **capital city** of Indonesia is Jakarta.

Largest cities

Jakarta is the largest city, with nearly eight-and-a-half million people. The second largest city is Surabaya and Bandung is the third largest city.

Head of country

Indonesia is ruled by a president and a **government**.

Population

There are over 200 million people living in Indonesia.

Money

The money in Indonesia is called the rupiah.

Language

The main languages spoken in Indonesia are Javanese, Sundanese, Malay and Madurese.

Religion

Most people in Indonesia are Muslims, some are Christian and a few are Hindu or Buddhist.

GLOSSARY

active (volcano) a volcano that still erupts

ashes burnt rock from a volcano

capital city the city where a country has its government

climate the average weather over a year

craft goods things that people have made themselves, to use or to sell

equator the line around the middle of the earth

erupt when a volcano erupts, hot rocks and lava burst out of its top and roll down its sides

extinct (volcano) a volcano that will never erupt again

government people who run a country

lava the hot rock that flows out of a volcano

martial arts sports where people learn how to defend themselves

monsoons winds that blow from different directions at different times of the year

paddy fields fields that are flooded, for growing rice

plot a small area of land

rainforest the natural forest in hot and wet tropical areas

shanty towns areas of poor housing in cities in poor countries

strait a narrow stretch of water between two areas of land

veranda a shady area outside a house, with a large overhanging roof

volcano a mountain made from lava

INDEX